THE ROYAL NAVY

1815—1915

T0346116

THE ROYAL NAVY

1815 — 1915

The Rede Lecture 1918

(1 June)

ADMIRAL
THE MARQUESS OF
MILFORD HAVEN

P.C., G.C.B., LL.D. &c.

CAMBRIDGE
AT THE UNIVERSITY PRESS
1918

CAMBRIDGE
UNIVERSITY PRESS

University Printing House, Cambridge CB2 8BS, United Kingdom

Published in the United States of America by Cambridge University Press, New York

Cambridge University Press is part of the University of Cambridge.

It furthers the University's mission by disseminating knowledge in the pursuit of
education, learning and research at the highest international levels of excellence.

www.cambridge.org
Information on this title: www.cambridge.org/9781107418677

© Cambridge University Press 1918

First published 1918
First paperback edition 2014

A catalogue record for this publication is available from the British Library

ISBN 978-1-107-41867-7 Paperback

THE ROYAL NAVY
1815—1915

WHEN, nearly four years ago, this terrible war broke out the British Navy, as a whole, had been at peace for a century. That is to say, we had not once been at war with a great maritime power with oversea possessions, which would have necessitated putting forth our entire naval strength everywhere. And yet hardly a year passed during this long span of time that did not see detached portions of the Royal Navy fighting somewhere on the globe, ashore or afloat.

During this century the navies of the world underwent the most profound changes in ships and their weapons since the long distant days when sails supplanted oars as the motive power*.

It will be of interest to trace both the

* Oars in addition to sails were used in galleys up to the end of the 18th century.

activity of, and these changes in, our navy in the interval between the two great wars.

Hard fighting on land and at sea was still going on in North America and the Atlantic during the year 1815, but so far as the navy was concerned the great European War had come to an end the year before.

Soon after the Peace Lord Exmouth, one of the veterans of the war, was sent out from England with a small squadron to deal finally with the Dey of Algiers and put an end to Christian slavery. Having been joined by a few Dutch frigates the admiral presented an ultimatum on arrival and then promptly engaged at close quarters the numerous forts defending Algiers. These were only silenced after a long day's fighting, lasting well into the night, with heavy losses in lives.

Ships are intended to fight ships, not forts, against which they are always at a disadvantage, which moreover the progress of science has steadily increased. From the first, the British Navy has only attacked forts when there were no ships to fight, but the results on the whole were not encouraging.

Only once, midway through this century, did the navy do any fighting in European waters and on a large scale*. This war, generally spoken of as the Crimean War, but which was also a Baltic War as far as the navy was concerned, furnished some examples of ships *versus* forts, undertaken *faute-de-mieux*. In both theatres of war the Russian ships found themselves greatly outnumbered by the allied fleets and, not unnaturally, preferred to remain behind the shelter of the guns of Sebastopol and Kronstadt. In the bombardment of Sebastopol, which was the preliminary act of the long siege, the ships got the worst of it.

In the Baltic the Anglo-French fleets, finding Kronstadt too strong, operated against Bomarsund in the first year and the following year attacked Sveaborg. The former was, after a futile bombardment, captured by French troops and naval bri-

* Except the isolated case of Navarino.

gades, whilst the latter was finally destroyed by mortar vessels.

During the Syrian War of 1840 St Jean d'Acre surrendered after a short bombardment by the fleet, which only suffered trifling losses. The guns of the forts had been prepared for a long-range action, and when the ships ran close in the guns could not be depressed sufficiently owing to the embrasures having been filled up from below for safety. The main magazine blew up very soon, after which the defence collapsed. The other coast-towns were taken by assault by men landed from the fleet, which included an Austrian and a Turkish squadron.

The only other bombardment on a considerable scale, by powerful ironclads, was that of Alexandria in 1882. The armament on both sides, except a few very heavy ship's guns, was nearly identical, having been turned out in the same English workshops. The decision was reached not so much by the destruction of the forts, which were poorly handled, as by their evacuation, after one or two magazines had blown up, and the ships did not suffer much.

During the wars with China and Burmah the navy did a good deal of bombarding, but the forts were mostly antiquated and badly fought. Many of these forts were taken by assault by sailors as well as soldiers. The same applies to the operations in the Paraná River in South America in 1845 and those in Japan in 1863.

The battle of Navarino in 1827 was the only fleet action fought during this long period. Like that of Lepanto in the same waters about 250 years earlier, but on a small scale, it was the battle of the Cross against the Crescent. Its peculiar feature was that it was fought out at anchor, the allied British, French and Russian squadrons having entered the bay where the Turkish fleet and transports lay, merely as a demonstration and not with the intention of attacking, as Nelson did at the Nile and Copenhagen. When suddenly started it turned out to be a very bloody affair; the allies had the preponderance in ships of the line, the Turks in frigates, but the Sultan's forces were eventually destroyed, and his oppressive sway over Greece was at an end.

Chinese War Junks, both Imperial and piratical, and armed Slave Dhows were after this date the only kind of vessel the navy had to encounter. The latter, mostly off the South East coast of Africa and in the Red Sea, often proved to be formidable opponents to the ships' row-boats, which used to be detached under young officers for weeks at a time from their ships to cruise under sail in search of slavers. This service went on continually up to the end of the nineteenth century and was a splendid school for those who eagerly volunteered for this active service on their own element. The prize bounty of £5 for every slave liberated was an additional attraction.

The navy did much fighting on rivers during these years, using every kind of craft, many of which were specially built for the occasion. Practically every African river and those of Burmah and China were repeatedly the scenes of naval operations.

In the first Burmese War in 1824 a small steamer, the *Diana*, belonging to the East India Company, rendered great services in towing gun- and mortar-boats up the Rangoon River. She was probably the first steamship to be used in war.

The most notable of these river expeditions was that of 1884/5, when Lord Wolseleys's army for the relief of Gordon at Khartoum had to be transported up the Nile with all its stores in hundreds of row-boats. Small steamers were also employed, and these as well as the whale-boats had to be dragged up the successive cataracts with incredible labour.

The most important part of the navy's fighting during the century under review was done by Naval Brigades of Seamen and Marines, operating generally in conjunction with troops. Such brigades fought in three wars in China, three wars in Burmah, two wars in New Zealand, on the coast of Syria, in the Crimea, on the shores of the Baltic, in the Indian mutiny, in Abyssinia and Perak, Egypt and the Soudan, in four wars in South Africa, and on numerous occasions in West and East Africa. They employed their own artillery in many original ways. These weapons, dragged by human beings and every species of animal, ranged from war rockets, which precipitated the fall of Magdala, to the siege-guns before Sebastopol.

On two occasions naval brigades took their own ships' guns into the field, and these were undoubtedly the forerunners of the heavy guns which have been playing so great a part in the present war in France and elsewhere.

The first occasion was the Indian mutiny, when Captain Peel took his frigate, the *Shannon*, up the river to Calcutta, left her tied to the bank and took his entire ship's company up country to the relief of Lucknow. He took with him six 68-pounders, two 8 in. howitzers and eight 24-pounders, all mounted on improvised carriages. The brilliant share of Peel's brigade in the suppression of the mutiny and his tragic death at the end are too well known to be repeated here.

The second occasion, in more recent times, was the outbreak of the Boer War, when the need for something heavier than an ordinary field-gun at once became apparent. Captain Percy Scott, who had just arrived in Simon's bay, at once set to work mounting 4·7 in., and later 6 in. guns, on carriages which could be dragged by large spans of oxen. The first of these guns took a prominent part in the defence of Ladysmith, the remainder joined the columns in the field. One pair of 4·7 in. guns covered close on 800 miles in 53 marching days, chasing De Wet. After the first year all the naval guns were taken over by the army and played a decisive part to the end.

In addition to all this fighting the navy was frequently called upon to exert moral force, sometimes as mediator, in the quarrels between other states. Naval officers, from Admirals down to Lieutenants commanding gunboats, often had to act on their own responsibility in far off places, and their rough-and-ready diplomacy generally succeeded. Lord Palmerston, when Foreign

Minister, once said that whenever he had a difficult case to deal with he sent a Post Captain with his ship and he generally settled the matter out of hand.

In 1818 the first of the numerous arctic expeditions set out, at first more concerned in discovering the North West Passage, than in reaching the pole. These proved themselves to be campaigns as arduous and as costly in lives and ships as many a war. The uncertainty of the fate of Franklin's expedition led to the despatch of a number of others. Antarctic expeditions were not undertaken until much later, though the shores of the South Polar Continent had been explored early in Queen Victoria's reign, and so had the Australasian coasts. The last of the South Polar expeditions, completed in this century, was to end in the tragic death of its leader, Robert Scott, after having reached the pole.

The natural history of the sea has also been explored by many expeditions. Of these the most comprehensive in plan and the most fertile in results was that of H.M.S. *Challenger*, 1872—1876.

We cannot close this review without some reference to the surveys which continuously occupied a small fleet of vessels specially staffed and equipped. These, working in every sea and on every shore, laboriously produced the charts now used in ships of all nationalities.

So much for the activity of the navy. Let us now examine briefly the changes brought about in it by the march of science.

When, a few years ago, the now famous *Dreadnought*, who was to give her old Elizabethan name to an entire class of new battleships all over the world, left Portsmouth harbour on her maiden trip, she passed within a stone's throw of the old *Victory* in which Nelson had fought and died just a century before. If, as was shown on a certain painting of the incident, the *Dreadnought* was preceded by a destroyer and followed by a submarine, whilst an airplane flew above, then this striking picture would show at a glance the changes which a century had wrought in the fighting navy.

The greatest of these changes was of course that of the motive power—steam, which came very soon, but was slow in supplanting sails and in developing. Even our steam ironclads (to use the early term) were fitted with masts and sails until the latter part of the last century. Theoretically the sails were to help the engines when the wind was fair. This top-hamper certainly did the opposite when the wind was foul; in action it would have been a source of danger.

The 120 32-pounder muzzle-loaders of the three-decker, firing a round solid shot with which a strong man could play a game of bowls, are replaced by the eight 15 in. breech-loaders of the *Queen Elizabeth*, which can make accurate shooting at 20,000 yards and over, with a projectile the size of a man and weighing over a ton.

The desire for greater power, which necessitated longer barrels, and for greater accuracy at the longer ranges, produced the breech-loading gun. Our first type of these suffered from the serious defect that the breech-block, only kept in place by friction,

16

often blew out when the gun was fired. This produced such distrust that we stuck to muzzle-loaders, constructing these up to 80 ton weight. We were a long way the last nation to adopt breech-loading guns.

As a defence against the long, pointed projectiles fired by a rifled gun the ships' sides were provided with armour, which gradually passed from thick, soft iron plates over small surfaces, to comparatively thin, hardened steel ones, spread over larger spaces. Steel had meanwhile taken the place of wood in ship construction, double bottoms and water-tight compartments were introduced.

The invention of the Whitehead or automobile torpedo, at first only carried in the small, very fast vessels specially designed for the purpose, was believed at the time to be bound to revolutionize naval warfare by sweeping the "Capital ship" off the seas. Manœuvres seemed to confirm this view, but subsequent war experience did not do so. The torpedo was a deadly enough weapon, but in practice it so rarely hit its mark, and it was not until carried by the submarine that it became the most deadly of all sea weapons. The torpedo boat, for its own safety, had to work at night, and the torpedo, which itself was unreliable in its behaviour, once launched overboard, could therefore as a rule not be fired off near enough to its target to ensure hitting. The submarine on the other hand, if it can only take up a suitable position in time, can approach its victim, unseen, so near that the torpedo is almost bound to hit its mark. As my hearers are probably aware, the torpedo is a small, self-propelled steel vessel, shaped somewhat like a shark. Its engines, which are worked by compressed air, stored in a separate compartment, drive propellers which nowadays give it a speed of about 40 knots. The torpedo, which can be set to run at any desired depth, carries in its head a charge which explodes on striking. Although greatly improved in speed and in ability to maintain a straight course it cannot compare with the gun in accuracy at long ranges when fired at a swiftly moving target. Having to force its way through the water it takes, roughly speaking, one minute to traverse the distance covered by a projectile fired from a gun in one second.

Still the moral effect of this new weapon, which was aimed at the most vulnerable portion of an ironclad's hull, was great. The French built large flotillas of torpedo-boats and this led in this country to the creation of the Torpedo-Boat-Destroyer, which eventually superseded the smaller torpedo-boat. The danger from torpedo attack was the direct cause of the construction of large artificial, completely enclosed harbours like those at Dover and Portland.

An attempt was also made to protect ships at anchor by steel nets hung round them, but these were never of real use since the torpedoes were always able to get through the nets by means of cutters fitted to their nose.

The evolution of the so-called "Capital Ship," or the ship fit to lie in the line of battle, as it used to be defined, was long drawn out. For many years the Channel

Fleet consisted only of "samples," sometimes built in twos or threes, but always changing.

The battleship of the present day, the so-called "Dreadnought-type," was a bold step in advance. She was designed (1) to carry as sole armament the largest number of the heaviest producible guns which could be mounted in revolving turrets on the upper deck, (2) to steam at the highest attainable speed. She was also given very complete armour protection. No existing battleship could stand up to her nor escape her. Every navy, except the smallest, copied the type.

The two factors—biggest gun and highest speed—are made progressive by science. This process began very soon. Displacement, that is length, breadth and draught of water, must be increased in proportion ; very soon it is found that dry docks and basins are not big enough, harbour entrances not deep enough, not to speak of the cost nor of putting too many eggs in one basket. If reports are true it looks as if, since the war began, we have progressed along that road to an alarming extent.

Together with this new battleship there appeared, in this country, an entirely new class of ship, which was given the very descriptive title of "Battle-Cruiser." In this case the two above-mentioned factors of gun and speed are reversed in their order. The speed was placed first, consequently the number of guns (of the same calibre as in the battleship) is reduced, and so is the thickness of the armour. In this type too it looks as if we had become seized by megalomania.

The tremendous power of the battle-cruiser was shown early in the war in the battle of the Falkland Islands. Since then these vessels have done most of the fighting, notably in the battle of Jutland, and on the Dogger Bank the year before. It may well be that, after the war, when the further development of the submarine will, as it undoubtedly must, profoundly affect the composition of the navy of the future, the battle-cruiser, though not in an exaggerated form, will be found among the survivors.

The early ironclads, which I have spoken

of as "samples," were all single-screw ships, but from frigates downwards paddles were in use in the early steam days. Twin screws were eventually applied to every class of vessel. Later, the water-tube boiler, allowing far greater steam pressures, displaced the old tank boiler. With this century came the turbine engine and the oil-fed boiler— a combination which made it possible to produce a cruiser with the phenomenal speed of the "saucy Arethusa," who so quickly made her name under the gallant Tyrwhitt.

Electricity has long ago taken the place of the " Purser's Dip " for internal lighting, while the condensing plant and the refrigerating room have made the rusty tank water and "salt horse " of my early days merely a tradition for the present generation.

The last scientific equipment to be added to the fighting ship, wireless telegraphy, has revolutionized naval strategy and profoundly affected tactics.

The methods of entry and training, both of officers and men, show immense changes since the days of *Midshipman Easy* and the Press Gang, under which the last great war was fought.

With the introduction of steam a special class of non-combatant officers, engineers, at first of warrant, then of commissioned, rank, grew up side by side with the executive officer. With the twentieth century a new scheme of common entry was introduced for both executive and engineer officers. This was mainly due to the desirability that all sea officers should be conversant with machinery, which had gradually been introduced into every form of the ship's activity. A contributory cause was a difficulty which had arisen as to the supply of engineer officers under the necessarily limited condition of their special calling.

As to the main cause: not only is the modern ship moved entirely by machinery, but her heavy guns are loaded and laid, the turrets trained, by machinery. The torpedo, part of all ships' armament, is both charged and run by machinery. Special engines are required for weighing and stowing the anchors, for hoisting in and out the heavy steamboats carried by ships, for steering the ship, for pumping water out of a ship, for the fire service, for search-lights and all internal lighting, for ventilation, for condensing water, for refrigerating provision-chambers and many other purposes.

By this scheme Engineering was added to the existing branches of Gunnery, Torpedo, Navigation, Wireless Telegraphy and Signalling, &c., in which a certain proportion of officers had for some years been specially trained. Gunnery and Torpedo Lieutenants had all along been in charge of the machinery of their respective departments, which included all electric machinery in the latter.

Ignorant criticism has condemned this scheme as producing "Jacks-of-all-trades" and "Masters of none." The exact opposite is the case. The young officers are all given most excellent, general naval training in all its branches. Later, a certain number of them, in the proportions required, acquire the "mastery" of one of its "trades." The scheme which enters boys at the age when they ordinarily leave the preparatory schools for the public ones, keeps them for four years at special colleges, before sending them to sea as midshipmen. There of course the training is continued, which aims at fitting the sea officers ultimately, after a period as assistants, (1) to command, (2) to navigate, (3) to fight any one of his H.M. ships. Judging by the results obtained so far this scheme promises very well indeed.

In one particular the scheme had to be altered: its originators had included Marine Officers in the common entry. It had not been sufficiently appreciated that the Royal Marines, a corps unique to this country, are essentially a military body, additionally trained to fight afloat. Their land and sea service, in peace, alternate, and the constantly changing Naval Officers, devoid of military training and tradition, could never have become real Marine Officers in barracks. The officers of this corps therefore continue to be entered separately, but they now receive a thorough naval training, like their men, and they render excellent service when embarked. In large ships for instance Marines man a proportion of the turrets, and in all ships some of the lighter guns. A great change from my early days when there was a common saying that the two most useless things in the ship were the Mizzen Royal (the smallest square sail) and the Marine Officer.

On the conclusion of the peace after the great war an immense reduction was at once made in the fleet in commission, and the seamen were "paid off," that is discharged, in their thousands. During the first half of the nineteenth century men were only entered for any ship fitting for sea and only for the term of the commission. Popular captains filled up their ships' companies much quicker than known martinets.

The greater complication of ships' armaments and fittings required special training, and eventually boys were entered in training ships, who then had to serve, first for 10 years, later increased to 12 years, from the rank of Ordinary Seamen at 18. Petty officers served longer and earned a pension. These, up to a certain age, formed a good reserve for war, but they had no rank and file behind them. At the age of 30, after excellent training and sea experience, an Able Seaman was discharged and, disappearing into private life, was lost to the navy. It was not until near the end of last century that this great wastage was realized. Since then every seaman, on leaving the active service, after 12 years' service, passes automatically into the Royal Fleet Reserve for a further period of service. Thanks to this the navy now possesses a large body of real reservists. A small number of short service men were then entered annually to build up this Reserve more quickly.

The Coast Guard consists of selected active service men of all ratings who, stationed round the coast, serve under the Board of Customs and the Board of Trade, chiefly for life-saving work in cooperation with the Lifeboat Institution. One half serve afloat every year for a few weeks during the Naval Manœuvres. The weak part of the scheme is that on mobilisation the whole body (except the small number required to man the Coast Signal Stations) join the fleet, and their important peace work collapses, since no substitutes are provided.

The so-called "Royal Naval Reserve," dating from about 1860, and recruited only in the Merchant Service, is really a partially trained auxiliary force, which has proved of immense service in this war, precisely for the mass of auxiliary service which has cropped up everywhere. The R. N. R. Officers on the other hand, who underwent much more effective training, have taken their place worthily by the side of the regular officers in every class of ship.

In 1864 an important change was made: the White Ensign became the sole flag of the navy, which up to then had used three different ones. As far back as the days before the Dutch Wars—about 300 years ago—when the fleet was assembled for war it used to be organized in three squadrons: Centre, Van and Rear. As the ships were numerous and very much alike in appearance it was found useful to distinguish them by different ensigns*. Thus the Centre, under the Admiral of the Fleet, flew the Red Ensign, the Van the White, and the Rear the Blue. In each squadron the Van was under a Vice-Admiral, the Rear under a Rear-Admiral. The flags of these admirals were of the colour of the respective ensigns, except that the Admiral of the Fleet flew the Union Flag, or Jack. There were thus nine grades of admirals in the fleet, and quite early in the eighteenth century, about the time when the need for coloured squadrons had disappeared, these flag officers were, curiously enough, given substantive rank as such. That meant that when a Captain was promoted to flag rank he first became " Rear-

* The same plan was followed in other large fleets, such as the French and the Dutch.

Admiral of the Blue," then "of the White," finally "of the Red"; the next step was "Vice-Admiral of the Blue" and so on. This plan remained in force until 1864, long after the navy was split up into many separate fleets and squadrons. In 1805, by which time the main fleet had ceased to be commanded by the Admiral of the Fleet, the separate rank of "Admiral of the Red" was created, presumably for the sake of symmetry. Retired flag officers used in those days to be spoken of as "Admirals of the Yellow." With the introduction of the White Ensign the nine classes of admirals were reduced to the present three, all flying the white flag with the St George's Cross. This change of ensign was directly due to the formation of the above-mentioned Royal Naval Reserve. As an inducement to join the force it was decided that ships commanded by R.N.R. Lieutenants and partly manned by R.N.R. men were to be privileged to fly the Blue Ensign*.

* Subsequently this was extended to the Supply and Auxiliary services.

As it was then, somewhat tardily, recognized by the Admiralty that the greatly reduced and scattered squadrons no longer required the complicated "coloured flag system" the Red Ensign was handed over, for sole use, to the merchant service (which had always flown it), and the remaining, white ensign became that of the Royal Navy.

Just fifty years ago, when I entered the navy, another, much appreciated change was made: compulsory shaving was abolished, and the bushy whiskers of the day grew into bushy beards; they were not kept clipped until much later. Nowadays clean shaving has set in as a fashion.

In those days uniform regulations were not very strictly carried out. In my first ship one of the lieutenants, who was a dandy, wore on his London-made uniforms an *oval* instead of the round curl on the distinction lace of the cuff. Another, who had been brought up in France, always wore a cap made exactly like a French

Képi with a horizontal peak. As no white coats were allowed, officers often wore in the tropics transparent alpaca coats of navy blue which the sun soon turned green. Tall white hats, suggestive of the Derby, were worn by some captains. Up to the time of the Crimean War captains often put their galley's crews into fancy rigs; in the *Tiger* they wore black and yellow striped jerseys, in the *Royal Oak* they had white oak wreaths embroidered round the edges of their blue collars in lieu of the three rows of braid. In the Mediterranean Captain Dundas's crew had Dundas tartan round their caps in place of the ribbon with the ship's name, whilst those of the *Vulture* had that bird embroidered in gold right across the front of their cloth jumpers.

The advent of a new century brought about a great change in the political outlook of the navy. For centuries our naval forces at home had been based on the South coast, with an eye on the old enemy across the Channel. Occasional spells of alliance did not affect this arrangement. Along the South coast, and continued round the Eastern corner to the Medway, were placed, behind coast defences, all our Dockyards and enclosed anchorages like Dover and Portland. Stores of all kinds—ammunition, coal, oil, victuals, &c.—were collected there; all the training establishments and schools for officers and men—Gunnery, Torpedo, Electricity, Engineering, &c.—also naval and marine barracks and hospitals, &c.

The new naval power which had arisen in the far corner of the North Sea began to assume formidable proportions with the opening years of the twentieth century, and it became increasingly clear with what object this new fleet was being built up so systematically. About the same time the old enemy on the other side of the Channel had gradually become a friend. Everything therefore pointed to an inevitable change of front for the navy from South to East— a tremendous undertaking. The conditions on that long East coast, prolonged by the

Orkneys, were not encouraging. On the English coast there are no harbours, except Harwich, and this was only suitable for small craft, for which it had already been in use for some time. The Humber is only a wide river mouth. The Scottish coast possesses two fine anchorages: the Forth and Cromarty, and these had been provided with some measure of defences. Nowhere did we have any government dry docks or ship-repair establishments, nor anything in the shape of a properly equipped naval base, but there were several private shipyards along the coast. Land was bought at Rosyth in the Forth, and a great naval establishment planned and begun. Work on this was spasmodic and had not progressed far when war came.

By comparison the German situation was very favourable. All her naval requirements—facilities for building, repairing and equipping every class of ship as well as protected anchorages—were concentrated in the inner corners of two adjacent seas, joined by a ship canal as well as by the longer route round the peninsula which divides the two seas. Entrance into the Baltic is confined to one, neutral, channel the Sound, only deep enough for light cruisers. The other two, deep water channels, the Belts are controlled by Germany.

In the North Sea the short coast-lines running North and West from the corner behind Heligoland are guarded by chains of small islands and all sea approaches are very shallow. It may here be pointed out that the value of Heligoland has been somewhat overrated. In the condition in which it was ceded to Germany in exchange for territory elsewhere it was of very little use for naval purposes. A small, round, flat-topped rock, it only afforded precarious anchorage in its lee. The Germans have converted it into a huge fort, and at great cost have made by its side a small artificial harbour for torpedo craft. Had we done this in our time it might have become a *casus belli.* As it is it is not far enough out for a real advance base for Germany, being only about one hour's steaming for a destroyer from the mainland. Besides which, coast defence guns are only dangerous within their range, like a watch-dog within the length of his chain. In war with France the Channel Islands formed a far more effective advance base for us.

In the autumn of 1913 the Admiralty decided to carry out, for the first time, a test mobilisation of the fleet in the following summer. The decision had to be made so far in advance as the expenses had to be included in the estimates for 1914/5, which were drawn up about November and presented to parliament early in the new year.

It should be explained that Naval mobilisation differs greatly from Military mobilisation inasmuch as the major portion of the fleet is kept permanently on a war footing. A ship in commission is fully manned and stored for three months; she can proceed on active service at a moment's notice.

The Reservists called up from civil employment on mobilisation are, in the army, required to raise existing peace units to war strength. In the navy they are merely required to do this for the minor portion of the fleet in Reserve with skeleton crews. This holds good in all countries. The proportion between the fully manned and the reserve ships varies in different countries, but the former always consists of the latest and best ships. In this country we had for some time back (as was generally known) introduced a system by which the Reserve Fleet was divided into two classes. The best of these ships were manned by so-called "Nucleus Crews," of sufficient strength to enable the ships to make short cruises and keep up their gunnery exercises. The balance of the crews were the while undergoing training or were otherwise employed in the three principal home ports—Portsmouth, Plymouth and Chatham—on which the ships were based. These men could at any time on an emergency be sent on board their ships whilst these were raising steam. These nucleus-crew ships were always kept fully stored.

A test mobilisation had never been carried

out as by law we are not allowed to call out Reservemen except when war is imminent. Hence for the test planned for 1914 Parliamentary sanction was necessary. It also entailed elaborate preparation. The Fleet-Reservemen were all in civil employment and the Admiralty had to come to an arrangement with their employers to set them free for a few weeks in the coming summer, undertaking if necessary to find temporary substitutes through the Labour Exchanges. Both the employers and the Reservemen responded readily to the call and by the first days of July the Admiralty was able, for the first time, to man the entire fleet as for war. R.N.R. personnel could of course only be taken from merchant ships which happened to be in home ports at the time.

Tactical exercises on an unprecedented scale were then carried out in the Channel after the fleet had been reviewed by H.M. the King on steaming out of Spithead. These had just been completed according to programme by the end of July and the re-assembled fleet was on the point of dispersing for de-mobilisation, when the political outlook took an alarming turn by Austria's ultimatum to Serbia. On the following Monday morning the fleet was to disperse, but on the Sunday the Admiralty, as a precautionary measure, ordered the ships to remain where they were until further orders. A few days later the mobilised fleet was sent to its war stations. What followed is common knowledge.

It may be said, broadly speaking, that the duty of any navy on the outbreak of war is, so far as possible, to find and destroy the enemy's ships. But there is a great difference between continental powers and island powers.

In the case of continental powers, which by the possession of sea coasts are also maritime powers, this action of the fleets which they maintain alongside of their great armies, is subsidiary to the military action.

In the case of an island kingdom like ours it is the primary and supremely important action which must necessarily precede all military action. An island exists only by means of its sea communications, and it is the paramount duty of its fleet at once to control these communications for the purpose of defence as well as of offence.

The sea must be denied to the enemy, (1) to prevent oversea attack and invasion directed against the island itself or any of its dependencies, (2) to stop his oversea trade by which the enemy could replenish his war material and otherwise enrich himself.

The sea must be kept open for our own use, (1) for the purpose of transporting military expeditions against the enemy's home or colonial territories, (2) for the purpose of keeping up our own supplies and oversea trade generally.

To this end the enemy's ships must be destroyed, or contained in his ports if they cannot be got at. Until this is done it is not considered safe to send troops across the sea. (This axiom did not apply to the sending of our Expeditionary Force across the Channel to France, though elaborate arrangements had to be made for its defence on transit.)

In this war however it was of such supreme importance for us to assemble all the troops we could for the help of France and Belgium that the risk, such as it was, had to be run. From the furthest corners of the earth military forces, including those furnished by the dominions, had to be escorted by the bulk of our cruisers, which normally should all have been employed in clearing the seas of enemy cruisers. These, especially in the Indian Ocean, were thus at first not much hampered in their war upon commerce, and effected as a consequence a certain number of captures. Thanks to the arrangements of our War Staff (which some critics affirmed to be non-existent) these losses in all seas were extremely small. In most cases they were directly due to the masters of the ships not obeying the Admiralty instructions.

In time of peace France kept large garrisons in her extensive North African possessions, which skirt the entire shores of the Western basin of the Mediterranean. On mobilisation these were urgently required in their home country, and had therefore to be transported across the intervening seas without loss of time. Italy being still neutral, the only danger to guard against at sea was the Austrian Navy, and this the superior French fleet, concentrated for some years in the Mediterranean, was fully able to do. But it so happened that when the war broke out the German battle cruiser *Goeben* and the fast light cruiser *Breslau* were at Pola, the Austrian military port in the Adriatic. These ships had been in the Mediterranean for a year or more. It also so happened that the French had at that time not built either battle cruisers or fast light cruisers, relying for war on their strength in armoured cruisers and large destroyers. Thanks to their great speed, much superior to anything the French possessed, these two enemy ships had it in their power seriously to interfere with, if not to stop, all troop movement across the Western Mediterranean. They did make one rush westward, the *Goeben* throwing some 11 in. shell into the Algerian town of Bona on the way (the kind of bombardment the inhabitants of Scarborough have had experience of) but it all came to nothing. It so happened that we had some battle cruisers and fast light cruisers in the Mediterranean at the time, and the Germans very soon found themselves so hunted that they utterly failed in their original object, never having even sighted a French transport. The narrow, neutral waters between Italy and Sicily, barred to our ships, were the enemy's first refuge, before escaping finally into the Greek Archipelago and up the Dardanelles. That these two ships, especially the *Goeben*, were not brought to action and destroyed will of course always remain a matter of great regret, for her presence at Constantinople had far-reaching consequences*. It was at least a great satisfaction for us to know that the important French troop movements across the Mediterranean were not delayed a minute or hampered in the slightest degree. The German scheme was obviously based on our being neutral.

* The *Breslau* has since been destroyed.

The outstanding feature of this war is undoubtedly the submarine and its rapid development. One of its peculiarities is that it is the only class of vessel that cannot be fought by its equal. For two submarines to set out and fight each other in the North Sea is like two men setting out from opposite sides of, say Wimbledon Common, in a very thick fog, with the same object. (Submarines which met accidentally have once or twice fought.)

For a long time past the navy has concentrated all its energy and ingenuity in finding means of destroying these pests of the sea. The first thing to do was to make our ships secure from attack at their anchorages. Submarine-proof obstructions for the defence of harbour mouths have long been in effective use. In confined waters, near our shores, very successful devices have hampered or kept away these craft altogether. In blue water submarines are most difficult to deal with, which is not to be wondered at, seeing that their normal condition is one of absolute invisibility.

The greatest danger to the submarine comes from the air; a bomb dropped within a certain distance of a submerged submarine is fatal to it.

The submarine's weak point is its slow speed when submerged. This makes very fast ships steering irregular courses practically immune. This defect is however being gradually overcome by larger displacement and more powerful engines. On the surface the newest enemy types have now, as I understand, a speed equal to that of battleships. These new submarines already carry a few guns of medium calibre, but these will certainly be increased in power and numbers as the displacement grows. Ultimately we shall see submersible cruisers, armed with guns and torpedoes, protected by armour, with a surface speed equal to any existing surface craft. (It must of course be understood that this great progress neither is, nor will by any means be, confined to the enemy's navy.) These new cruisers will require attendant vessels as "Eyes," for offence and defence, the same as the fleets now, but in the air, not on the water.

It is quite possible to build a ship which is practically unsinkable by mine or torpedo, but this entails certain sacrifices in other directions.

Unsinkable and submersible merchant steamers, at least for certain essential or valuable cargoes, would appear to be inevitable for the future, notwithstanding the increased cost and decreased cargo space.

The Air Force is now distinct from Army and Navy, but it was the Navy which started the Seaplane, developed it and made, and continues to make, such splendid use of it. It is difficult to forecast its future, but still greater assimilation to the seabird, at home in both elements, appears not unlikely.

We cannot conclude this short comparison of war conditions 100 years apart, without some reference to the merchant navy. The fleets of Howe, St Vincent and Nelson were largely self-supporting. Water, like coal and oil in our days, was their only, ever recurring need, and as it could not be brought to them the ships had to fetch it themselves. For all other purposes a few victuallers and store ships sufficed. Transports were only required for comparatively small military forces. The bulk of the mercantile navy was free to attend to its business, but privateers made many captures up to the end.

In this war the naval and military supply and transport services, including hospital ships, permanently require about one-half of the merchant tonnage. These, as well as the trading ships, are constantly exposed to the attacks of the ruthless submarines with gun and torpedo, and the ever-increasing danger from mines. Over 12,000 of these merchant seamen have already lost their lives, but the survivors are as undaunted and intrepid as ever. The existence of this country now literally depends on the faithful services of these men, and

I cannot help feeling that the merchant navy, which has been linked up with the Royal Navy as never before, has by now earned for itself the right to wear on its colours the Red Cross of St George, the old fighting flag of England.

Nor must we forget the services of all those brave men, mostly fishermen, who are serving in the mine-sweeping and patrol vessels of all kinds along our coasts, so many of whom have already given their lives in this dangerous service.

We have seen how greatly the fleets in the last great war differed from those fighting now—on the water, under the water and in the air. This difference however is only in the instruments of sea warfare. The spirit of those who use these new ships and weapons has proved itself to be the same as that which animated the British Navy in the days of Drake, Blake, Hawke, Rodney and Nelson.